Happy Earth Day!

By Deborah Hopkinson

Illustrated by Jennifer Zivoin

The editors would like to thank Gerald Torres, professor of environmental justice at the Yale School of the Environment and board chair of earthday.org, for his assistance in the preparation of this book.

A GOLDEN BOOK • NEW YORK

Text copyright © 2023 by Deborah Hopkinson
Cover and interior illustrations copyright © 2023 by Jennifer Zivoin
All rights reserved. Published in the United States by Golden Books, an imprint of Random House Children's Books, a division of Penguin Random House LLC, 1745 Broadway, New York, NY 10019. Golden Books, A Golden Book, A Little Golden Book, the G colophon, and the distinctive gold spine are registered trademarks of Penguin Random House LLC.
rhcbooks.com
Educators and librarians, for a variety of teaching tools, visit us at RHTeachersLibrarians.com
Library of Congress Control Number: 2021947514
ISBN 978-0-593-56669-5 (trade) — ISBN 978-0-593-56670-1 (ebook)
Printed in the United States of America
10 9 8 7 6 5 4 3 2

It's big and round. It gives us fresh air to breathe and clean water to drink. It gives us good, rich dirt to grow our food.

Birds soar in its skies. Dolphins play in its oceans.

What is it? Earth, of course! And did you know there's a special day to thank our planet?

Let's find out about Earth Day!

Before we had an Earth Day, people in America weren't taking good care of the environment.

Factories spewed stinky smoke into the sky and dumped garbage into rivers, lakes, and streams. Fumes from cars, trucks, and buses made the air gray—and hard to breathe.

Farmers sprayed pesticides to kill unwanted bugs in their fields. But these chemicals hurt animals and birds, too. Even the bald eagle, the symbol of our nation, was in trouble.

Then, in 1969, a company drilling for oil off the coast of California didn't pay attention to safety. Three million gallons of oil spilled into the ocean and spread for miles.

People rushed to clean greasy seabirds. Volunteers worked to remove thick, smelly gunk from the sandy beaches.

When Gaylord Nelson, a United States senator from Wisconsin, saw the oil spill, it gave him an idea. What if there was one day when everyone in America came together to learn about nature? What if there was one day devoted to helping our planet?

Senator Nelson hired a student named Denis Hayes to organize it. They called the idea Earth Day. Denis has worked to protect the environment ever since!

The first Earth Day was held on April 22, 1970. Twenty million people in cities and towns all over America took part. They planted trees and picked up litter from roads, parks, and beaches.

Thousands marched in the streets calling for stronger rules against smoky air, dirty rivers, and oil spills.

Right from the start, Earth Day was a huge success!

Earth Day showed that people cared about the environment. America's leaders began to make new laws to help keep our air and water clean. They formed the Environmental Protection Agency to protect nature and people's health.

New rules kept factories from dumping so much into rivers. Farmers found ways to grow crops without using pesticides. Companies invented better car engines to keep the air cleaner.

Earth Day also helped people realize that some species of plants and animals were in danger of disappearing.

In 1973, the Endangered Species Act was passed. There's still much to be done, but hundreds of species, including whooping cranes, American crocodiles, gray wolves, and bald eagles, have already been saved from extinction.

In 1990, Earth Day went global. And in 2020, on Earth Day's fiftieth birthday, a *billion* people in more than 190 countries got involved!

Earth Day is the largest celebration on our planet. And that's good, because Earth needs us more than ever.

Humans have caused a big problem for Earth called global warming, or climate change. When we burn coal and oil to heat houses or make cars go, carbon dioxide is released. This invisible gas gets trapped in a layer above Earth. The layer keeps heat in and makes our planet warmer.

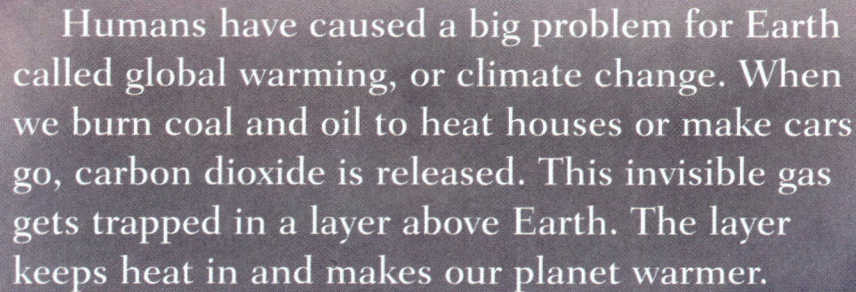

Climate change causes more severe storms, heat waves, and wildfires. Animals such as polar bears and penguins are in trouble because their icy homes are melting.

Earth Day brings people together to help fight climate change. One way to do this is to plant trees. Trees take in carbon dioxide and use it to grow. This keeps the harmful gas out of the air and helps reduce global warming.

It will take a lot of work to heal our Earth and protect all living things. But you can help!

On Earth Day, why not join with family and friends to plant trees in your community?

Plastic waste is another problem for our Earth. Plastic often ends up in the ocean, where it hurts fish, marine animals, and the water. On Earth Day, you can volunteer to collect plastic trash in your neighborhood or in a nearby park.

You can also help by recycling and using less plastic at home. Drink from a reusable water bottle. Use paper straws. And remind your family and friends to bring their own bags to the store.

Here are more ways you can help the Earth:

Compost

Decaying food in dumps and landfills gives off carbon dioxide and adds to global warming. Composting helps reduce food waste—and also makes our gardens grow. Here's how to get started:

Put organic food waste, such as vegetables, fruit, and eggshells, in a covered bowl or container in the kitchen.

When it's full, empty the container into a bin with a cover and keep it outside.

Add grass clippings and dead leaves. Mix it and let it sit.

If you start your compost bin on Earth Day, by the next April you'll have rich soil that is perfect for growing vegetables and flowers!

Make a Bug Hotel

You can make a bug hotel to give shelter to helpful insects, like ladybugs. Here's how:

Have an adult cut out a square from one side of a milk carton.

Fill the carton with twigs, pine cones, grass, leaves, and moss.

Place your bug hotel in a sheltered corner of your yard, on a balcony, or outside your apartment building. After a few days, check to see who has moved in!

Plant Flowers

Have you seen bees buzzing around flowers to gather nectar? Bees are important pollinators. They help us grow delicious fruits and vegetables, like apples, blueberries, pumpkins, and pears.

You can support bees by planting flowers in your yard, a community garden, or outside your school or church—just be sure to get permission before planting any seeds.

Grow Your Own Snack

You can grow baby carrots inside on a sunny windowsill! Fill a pot about eight inches deep with moist soil. Sprinkle baby carrot seeds on top and gently cover them with a little soil. Water often so that the soil stays moist. Be patient! Carrots can take three weeks to sprout.

When the seedlings are about two inches tall, thin them so there's an inch of space between each plant. It's easy! Use tiny scissors to snip off the stems or gently pull out extra seedlings.

In about sixty days, you'll see colorful carrot tops poking out. Pull up your carrots, wash them, and start munching!

Earth Day comes each April 22. But you don't have to wait for Earth Day to thank our planet. Earth's gifts are everywhere—you just need to look around and pay attention.

Visit a park or take a nature walk. Stop and smell a flower. Listen to the wind whisper in the trees. Watch clouds sailing in the sky. How many different kinds of birds can you see today?

When you pop a fresh strawberry into your mouth, think of the sun, rain, and soil that helped make it grow.

Remember—whether you plant a tree, use less plastic, start a compost bin, or care for baby carrots on a windowsill, you can help our planet. Together, let's make every day Earth Day!

Would your family like to find out more about Earth Day?

Visit earthday.org.